JEWISH
EARLY CHRISTIANITY

David Flusser

JEWISH SOURCES IN EARLY CHRISTIANITY

MOD Books   Tel-Aviv

JEWISH SOURCES IN EARLY CHRISTIANITY
by
DAVID FLUSSER

English translation by John Glucker

Second Printing – November 1993

English Series Editor: Shmuel Himelstein

ISBN 965-05-0466-4

Computerized phototypesetting & printing: Naidat Press Ltd.
Printed in Israel

MOD Books — P.O.B. 7103, Tel-Aviv 61070, ISRAEL

The messianic family tree as depicted in a monastery of the end of the twelfth century. The family tree begins with Boaz, continues through King David, and culminates in Jesus. Thus, according to Christian belief, this exemplifies the link between the Jewish and Christian Bibles.

Contents

Preface

THE SUBJECT OF THIS BOOK IS THE JEWISH SOURCES OF EARLY Christianity, with special attention to Christianity as reflected in the Gospels and in other books of the New Testament.

The study of the Jewish background of these works is relevant to Judaism itself, since it is likely to enrich our knowledge of the beliefs and opinions of the Jewish people during the period of the Second Temple, and to teach us something about Jewish spiritual creativity during those days, even in certain cases where our own information on such matters is meager.

We shall be saying nothing new if we maintain that Jesus was a Jew in every way. The Gospels have preserved his maxims and sayings, and thus it is not only the views and opinions of Jesus himself that have been preserved for us, but also details concerning the Jews of those days, especially concerning the world-view of the Sages, as well as information concerning the various streams in Judaism during the period of Jesus' life and activities.

The books of the New Testament contribute greatly to our knowledge of the Jewish Midrash (Biblical exegesis) of those days, and of the prevalent methods of studying the Bible. A comparison with the material we find in the New Testament also teaches us the extent to which the Dead Sea Sect influenced its Jewish environment, both in Palestine and abroad.

In the Book of Revelations of John, the last book of the New

Testament, we have early witnesses of Jewish eschatology and apocalyptics. The whole of the New Testament reflects the various Jewish beliefs and views concerning the final redemption, faith, and Messianism.

In the course of my lectures, delivered on the University Series of the Israel Army Radio Network, I have tried to expand, through an investigation of the books of the New Testament, our knowledge of the extensive flowering of Jewish spiritual life during the period of the Second Temple.

David Flusser
Jerusalem, 1987

I.

The Early Christian Writings and Their Relationship to Judaism
Hebrew

THE EARLY CHRISTIAN WRITINGS REFLECT IDEAS, BELIEFS, views and trends in Second Temple Judaism. They reflect the world of the Sages, including the Sages' Biblical exegesis, their parables, and even their own uncertainties. One also finds expressions of the hope for redemption and of the Messianic beliefs current in Judaism during that period. One can also discern echoes of most streams in Judaism of the time, including those of groups which the Sages regarded as heretical, such as Hellenistic Judaism and the Essenes, or the Dead Sea Sect. *Greek*

Jewish sources alone cannot teach us enough about Second Temple Judaism. Our information on Rabbinic Judaism from these sources, for example, dates from a few generations after the rise of Christianity. The Sages began to chronicle their own history only after the destruction of the Second Temple (70 C.E.), and most of those who recorded the earlier oral tradition in the Midrashim (books of Biblical exegesis) and in the rabbinic legends lived at least a generation after the destruction of the Temple or later. Nevertheless, even the superficial reader of these sources will soon find that they reflect an oral tradition which is in many cases considerably earlier than the period of those in whose names it is reported.

Early Christian literature thus reflects the world of the Sages at an earlier stage than its reflection in the Jewish sources. It reflects Jewish life in the Hellenistic diaspora, details of which we otherwise know chiefly from the writings of Philo of Alexandria. We can also learn from it about other Jewish diasporas and about Jewish customs which have not been recorded in early Jewish sources. Take an example: the Jewish custom of giving a boy his name during his circumcision ceremony is not known in our Talmudic literature, but in one of the Gospels (Luke 1:59–64) we are told that John the Baptist's father gave him his name during this ceremony. Or another example: the custom of passing around the glass of wine during the Kiddush (the blessing on the wine ushering in Sabbath and Holy Day meals) is unknown in the Talmudic sources, but the New Testament tells us that during the Last Supper Jesus asked that his cup should be passed among his Apostles (Luke 22:17 and parallel passages).

An investigation of this period, for which no Midrashic or Talmudic sources have reached us, also enables us to determine the form of some sayings of the Sages which is closest to the original. Where we find a saying both in a later Jewish source and in the New Testament, the most original form of the saying is the one we find in the earlier source – that is, in the New Testament. At the same time, we must not forget that the language of the New Testament was also influenced not only by controversies which originated in tensions inside Judaism itself, but also by the redactors of the Gospels, who in the Greek versions even changed the words of Jesus himself.

The three Gospels of Matthew, Mark, and Luke are closely interrelated due to their common sources and their mutual influence on one another. These three Gospels, which narrate the life of Jesus, are far more valuable as historical documents than the Gospel of John. The latter is not a historical document: Jesus is used there mainly as a means for spreading the ideas of John, the author of that Gospel.

The Greek redactions of the Gospels which have reached us clearly contain changes and alterations from the original versions. In those original versions, the Jewish character was far more clearly reflected than in the later redactions. Even the Epistles in the New Testament, which reflect the second stage of Christianity represented by the personality of Paul, bring out some important chapters in the history of Israel during those days, especially the spiritual history of Israel.

The spoken languages among the Jews of that period were Hebrew, Aramaic, and to an extent Greek. Until recently, it was believed by numerous scholars that the language spoken by Jesus' disciples was Aramaic. It is possible that Jesus did, from time to time, make use of the Aramaic language. But during that period Hebrew was both the daily language and the language of study. The Gospel of Mark contains a few Aramaic words, and this was what misled scholars. Today, after the discovery of the Hebrew Ben Sira (Ecclesiasticus), of the Dead Sea Scrolls, and of the Bar Kokhba Letters, and in the light of more profound studies of the language of the Jewish Sages, it is accepted that most people were fluent in Hebrew. The Pentateuch was translated into Aramaic for the benefit of the lower strata of the population. The parables in the Rabbinic literature, on the other hand, were delivered in Hebrew in all periods. There is thus no ground for assuming that Jesus did not speak Hebrew; and when we are told (Acts 21:40) that Paul spoke Hebrew, we should take this piece of information at face value.

This question of the spoken language is especially important for understanding the doctrines of Jesus. There are sayings of Jesus which can be rendered both into Hebrew and Aramaic; but there are some which can only be rendered into Hebrew, and none of them can be rendered only into Aramaic. One can thus demonstrate the Hebrew origins of the Gospels by retranslating them into Hebrew.

It appears that the earliest documents concerning Jesus were written works, taken down by his disciples after his death. Their language was early Rabbinic Hebrew with strong undercurrents of

Biblical Hebrew. Even in books of the New Testament which were originally composed in Greek, such as the Pauline Epistles, there are clear traces of the Hebrew language; and the terminology in those books of the New Testament which were composed in Greek is often intelligible only when we know the original Hebrew terms. In these books, we can trace the influence of the Greek translation of the Bible side by side with the influence of the Hebrew original.

Jesus was a Jew, faithful to Jewish Law. From his sayings, one can glean lost information about the world of his teachers, the Jewish Sages. In the Book of Revelation, the last of the books of the New Testament, written by a Palestinian, Greek-speaking Jew (whose Greek was somewhat imperfect), we can find a reflection of the Jewish vision of the end of days and of redemption. In the other books of the New Testament, we can also identify among the Jewish beliefs a strong yearning for redemption. This view assumed a new significance in Christianity.

II.

The Background of Jesus' Life

ONE CAN STATE WITH CERTAINTY THAT JESUS' PERSONALITY was outstanding in the Judaism of his period. It is true that our sources concerning Jesus are either Christian or derived from a familiarity with the Christian tradition. But a similar phenomenon is also true in relation to the Jewish sources: we have no information from non-Jewish sources even about such illustrious Jewish personalities as Rabbi Akiva or Rabbi Judah the Patriarch; and if Rabbi Akiva is mentioned by some of the Church Fathers, it is because they learned about him from the Jews.

Let us mention two Jewish sources about Jesus:

a. The conversation between Rabbi Eliezer Ben Hyrcanus and Jacob, the disciple of Jesus, which appears in the Talmudic literature (sources in *The Hebrew Encyclopedia* XX, p. 433). After the destruction of the Temple, Rabbi Eliezer was arrested by the Roman authorities and accused of being a Christian, but acquitted. He lived in Lydda, where a Christian community had existed from the very beginnings of Christianity (see Acts 9:32). Later on, he asked himself what he had done to warrant having been arrested as a Christian. This was the transition period from sympathy to hostility between Judaism and Christianity. He then remembered that he had once expressed pleasure at a saying of Jesus which he had heard from a disciple of Jesus named Jacob.

b. Josephus Flavius tells us in his *Antiquities of the Jews* (XX, 200–203) about the execution of Jacob, Jesus' brother. Jacob was executed in 62 C.E. by a Sadducee high priest, and we are told that he was the brother of Jesus, who was called Christ (= Messiah). Moreover, there is a passage extant in all the manuscripts of Josephus (*Antiquities*, XVIII, 63–64), which tells us that Jesus was more than merely human. This may, of course, be a piece of rewriting or plain forgery, and there are those who believe that the whole passage is a forgery interpolated into the text of Josephus.

The late Professor Victor A. Tcherikover, an expert on Second Temple history, pointed to the end of that passage, which reads: "And unto this day there are still people who are called Christians." It is unlikely, he argued, that such a sentence would be a forgery, and it appears that these are the words of Josephus himself. The question remained undecided until Professor Shlomo Pines found a different version of Josephus' testimony in an Arabic version of the tenth century: "At this time there was a wise man who was called Jesus, and his conduct was good, and he was known to be virtuous. And many people from among the Jews and the other nations became his disciples. Pilate condemned him to be crucified and to die. And those who had become his disciples did not abandon their loyalty to him. They reported that he had appeared to them three days after his crucifixion, and that he was alive. Accordingly they believed that he was the Messiah, concerning whom the Prophets have recounted wonders."

This testimony is entirely different from what we find in the Greek manuscripts of Josephus which have reached us. There, we are told that Jesus was executed at the recommendation of the leaders of the Jews. This accusation blaming the Jews for the death of Jesus is missing in the Arabic version. Nor does it say that he *was* the Messiah, as the Greek manuscripts have it, but that his disciples regarded him as the Messiah after he appeared to them, as they believed, and *they* considered him as the Messiah, "concerning whom the Prophets have recounted wonders." And indeed, if we look, for example, at what Isaiah says concerning the Messiah, we shall find there many wonderful things told about him. We should, therefore, assume that the Arabic text, which contains no trace of a Christian view, is what Josephus himself wrote concerning Jesus. One should understand from this that Josephus' attitude to the early Christians was favorable. Apart from Jesus, he mentions with sympathy the death of his brother James; and it may be no accident that Josephus also tells us about John the Baptist (*Antiquities* VII, 117).

The Hebrew name for Jesus, Yeshu, is evidence for the Galilean pronunciation of the period, and is in no way abusive. Jesus was a Galilean, and therefore the *a* at the end of his name, Yeshua, was not pronounced. His full name was thus Yeshua. In the Talmudic sources, which are from a later period, there is reference to a Rabbi Yeshu, who is not to be confused with Jesus.

According to Christian tradition, Jesus was born in Bethlehem and grew up in Nazareth, a small town mentioned in Hebrew literature and in the early medieval Hebrew poetry as a place occupied by priestly families after the destruction of the Temple. He grew up in a Jewish house and learned the sayings of the Sages. He was not a rabbi himself, although he was called Rabbi. At the age of thirty, he left his home and met John the Baptist. Both the New Testament and Josephus testify to the tremendous influence of John the Baptist on the people.

Jesus went through the ceremony of baptism together with other Jews (Luke 3:21). There is no Christian element in his baptism by John. As much as we can ascertain, Jesus himself never baptized anyone. Baptism entered Christian practice only after his death. Jesus stayed for a while in the company of John the Baptist, and then founded his own separate community. The reason for this separation was apparently Jesus' view of the Kingdom of Heaven as being realized here and now, as against the view of John the Baptist, which regarded the realization of Jewish Messianic aspirations as a future event.

Jesus founded a community and appointed twelve apostles, representing the twelve tribes of future Israel (Luke 22:30 and parallel passages), in order to spread his message that the Kingdom

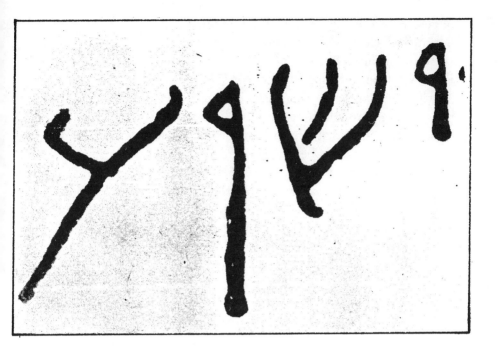

The word "Yeshu" (Jesus) in the ancient Hebrew script.

◀ *Capernaum. Ruins of the Roman era buildings.*

of Heaven was being realized. He attempted to return to Nazareth, but was rejected by his compatriots. He then went to Kfar Nahum (= Capernaum), where the mother-in-law of his great disciple Peter was living. He stayed there for some time and carried on his activities in that area. One insoluble question is the discrepancy between the chronology of the first three Gospels and that of the Gospel of John. According to John, Jesus had already been active for three or four years before deciding to go to Jerusalem; according to the first three Gospels, this period lasted only a few months.

His arrival in Jerusalem was motivated by two considerations: a) the approaching Passover; b) the desire to prevent the destruction of the Temple. Jesus came to warn the people and to call them to repentance. In Jerusalem, he did not engage, as before, in healing the sick and in working miracles. He did not clash with the Romans, but he did with the Sadducee leadership of the Temple, the families of the High Priests. This clash was caused by his attacks on them and by his prophecies of the destruction of the Temple. In that same era – forty years before the actual destruction of the Temple – we are told that Rabban Yohanan Ben Zakkai also prophesied its destruction.

No, He was resurrected

Jesus was captured by the Sadducees, handed over to the Romans, and executed by crucifixion on the orders of Pilate. His disciples later believed that he came back to life, and this story of the resurrection helped them to overcome the crisis through which they were going. They believed in him as the Messiah, and thus established the first Christian community in Jerusalem.

Jesus did not come to Jerusalem to proclaim his Messiahship. One of the crucial problems which cannot be solved is whether Jesus saw himself as the Messiah. Many Jewish scholars tend too simply to take this for granted. The New Testament documents lend support to the view of Christian scholars that Jesus did not regard himself as the Messiah. In what concerns us, suffice it to say that Jesus may have thought he was the Messiah. *No, He knew He was*

One should view Jesus against his Jewish background, the world of the Sages, to recognize and appreciate his great influence on those around him. Only thus shall we be able to understand how

Christianity was formed. Jesus was part and parcel of the world of the Jewish Sages. He was no ignorant peasant, and his acquaintance with the Written and the Oral Law was considerable.

For this reason, the sayings of Jesus are also an important source for our knowledge of the world of the Jewish Sages. Similarly, his relations with John the Baptist, who was connected with the Essenes, enable us to ascertain the Essene component in his doctrines. A study of the sayings of Jesus also paves the way toward an understanding of the Oral Law and of the Jewish Midrashim.

III.

The Written Law, the Oral Law, and Jesus

JESUS WAS A JEW WHO ADDRESSED HIMSELF ONLY TO JEWS, AND refused even to heal Gentiles. We have the touching story of the Roman centurion of Capernaum who came to Jesus asking him to heal one of his servants (Matthew 8:5; Luke 7:1–10). Jesus had to be convinced that the man was a benefactor of the Jewish people and had even built a synagogue. The Roman knew that Jesus wanted no contact with Gentiles, and he therefore declared that he was not worthy of coming under his roof. The New Testament, of course, does not provide the reason for his statement. The Roman believed that the healing rabbi was not allowed to enter the sick man's house because of the defilement of the Gentiles. He therefore advised Jesus to heal from a distance. Jesus healed the sick man, and we are told in that story that Jesus commented on the behavior of the Roman by saying: "I tell you, not even in Israel have I found such faith."

Jesus lived in a Jewish world which was flourishing within the framework of the Written Law (the Bible) and the Oral Law (what later became the Talmud). Many Christian scholars – with whom I disagree – believe that the keeping of the commandments consti- *just these* tuted a problem for Jesus. It is true that in the New Testament we *added* have some disputes ascribed to Jesus concerning the keeping of *by leaders* some particular commandments. But these disputes touch on minutiae. For example, in Mark (7:1–3), a Gospel which already shows a tendency toward separation from Judaism, we are told that some Pharisee Sages claimed that Jesus' disciples were not scrupulous enough in washing their hands before a meal. But it is well known that it was only in Jesus' time that this custom of washing one's hands before a meal became a general Jewish custom.

The same applies to healing the sick on the Sabbath. We cannot find in the first three Gospels any act of healing on the Sabbath, which was forbidden according to Jewish law of the period. Healing through speech was permitted even in cases where it was not a matter of life and death, and any healing was permitted in cases of life and death. The only case where Jesus appears to violate the laws of the Sabbath is where his disciples pluck ears of corn and pull out the seeds (Luke 6:1–6 and parallel passages). But in two secondary sources – one Jewish-Christian and one Christian – we are told that the disciples did not pluck the ears, but simply held them and pulled out the seeds by rubbing them with their hands. In this matter, there was a controversy between the Galileans, who regarded this as permissible on the Sabbath when using one's hands, and other Sages, who ruled that it was permissible only when one used one's fingers. It appears that the disciples of Jesus the Galilean followed the ruling of the Galilean Rabbi Judah bar Ilai.

Jesus was scrupulous in keeping the Jewish commandments. It is to be expected that the New Testament documents, written as they were in times of tension between Judaism and the Church, made a point of emphasizing that Jesus was on the side of those who abolished, partly or wholly, the commandments of the Torah. For example, in the story about the washing of the hands, we have a quotation from Isaiah concerning "teaching as doctrines the commandments of men" (Mark 7:7), where the quotation is taken from the Greek translation of Isaiah, and we can already detect a foreign influence in it. The whole passage is influenced by the doctrines of Paul, and it therefore expresses an apparent contradiction between the words of the living God as they appear in the

Bible and the tradition of the Elders of the Jews (Mark 7:8).

This raises the problem whether Jesus did away with the rulings of the Sages and put an emphasis only on the Written Law. This idea, which appears later in the writings of the Church Fathers, contains an absurdity – for if that had been the case Jesus would have been close to the Sadducees, and we know that he was in no way close to them. It is also clear that had Jesus lived only by the dictates of the Written Law, he would have been more stringent in certain areas (as were the Sadducees) in which we know that he was not stringent at all, and in which the Sages, too, were not stringent. When we examine Jesus' position on matters of Jewish Law, it appears that on some things he accepted the view of the more stringent authorities – the School of Shammai – and on the others, especially on matters of ideology, he was closer to the School of Hillel, whose motto was "Thou shalt love thy neighbor as thyself."

Jesus also opposed any excessive hairsplitting, and preferred to uphold the moral point of view. In matters of divorce, for example, he was as stringent as the School of Shammai (so in Matthew 5:32; 19:3-9). From unpublished research by Professor Shmuel Safrai it appears that in this matter the School of Shammai took the more stringent view because of its special consideration for the woman. The attitude of the School of Hillel was more liberal – but only toward the man. The School of Shammai looked after the woman's interest in other cases as well.

According to Matthew, Jesus adopted the point of view of the School of Shammai in order to justify the indissolubility of marriage in the case of fornication. On the same point, the position of the Essenes, who did not permit marriages to be dissolved in any case, was later incorporated into the New Testament – but that was already under the influence of Paul, who was indirectly related to the Essenes.

Here Jesus accepted the position of the School of Shammai as a matter of practical Jewish Law and not for the theocentric reasons which were typical of that School. In his attitude to people, on the other hand, he was closer to the School of Hillel, and the love of man was central to his teaching. His acceptance of the more stringent rulings of the School of Shammai had its origin in his fear of sin and his desire that man should live in an atmosphere of perfect holiness. Thus Jesus formed a bridge between the positions of the School of Hillel and the School of Shammai.

Jesus regarded the Torah, with all its jots and tittles, as a world complete in itself, on which the existence of the real world depended (Matthew 5:17–20), and he was therefore faithful to the Torah in its entirety. Like many members of the School of Hillel, Jesus gave the Torah a humanitarian explanation, at the same time taking the view that the smallest commandment weighed as heavily as the greatest. It is precisely the small commandments which he identified with the moral ones, sharing the view of the Sages and the Hasidim (the "Pious"). By being more stringent in moral matters, he wanted to develop the moral and humanitarian side of Judaism.

In the Sermon on the Mount (Matthew 5:17–18), Jesus interpreted the words of the Torah according to the more stringent moral sense, like the adherents of Rabban Yohanan ben Zakkai who stressed the moral side of Judaism. These more stringent interpreters were humane people, and that was why Rabban Yohanan quoted their views. The expression "stringent interpreters" in this context refers to people who were more stringent on moral commandments from an *a fortiori* point of view: the "minor" commandments are as important as the "major" ones; and one should be as scrupulous in keeping the moral commandments as one is in keeping the ritual ones.

Jesus' position is made clear in the fifth chapter of Matthew. There he speaks of keeping the Torah without transgressing against a jot or tittle. Anyone transgressing against the least commandment will not enter the Kingdom of Heaven, and anyone who keeps the "minor" commandments and teaches others to keep them shall be called great in the Kingdom of Heaven. He emphasizes that the righteousness of his disciples in keeping the commandments must be greater than that of the scribes, or else they shall not enter the Kingdom of Heaven. This more stringent position is exemplified thus: From the commandment "Thou shalt not kill," it follows that one should not be angry with others, for anger leads to killing. From the commandment "Thou shalt not commit adultery," it follows that even he who glances at a married woman with desire is like someone who has committed adultery in his heart. Jesus seems to repeat the view of the Jewish Sages, that the word "commit adultery" has four letters in Hebrew, since a man commits adultery with his eyes, hands, heart and feet (Matthew 5:27–30; and Mark 9:43–48).

The Christian sources, of course, provide us with the contrast between Jesus and Jewish Law. Matthew presents the views of Jesus as opposed to the views of the Sages. The truth of the matter, however, is that there is no difference between the views of Jesus and authentic Jewish traditions.

The Sermon on the Mount helps us to understand the Judaism of Jesus' time, and opens an avenue for understanding an important trend in the world of the Sages. We have before us a group of people who combined the demand for stringency in moral matters with love for their fellow men. This view is represented by Jesus, but what we find here is not a doctrine which is peculiar to himself.

IV.

Jesus' Polemic Against the Pharisees

THE PROBLEM OF JESUS' ATTITUDE TOWARDS THE PHARISEES
has not in the past been accorded the clear elucidation it deserves.
Some Jewish scholars wished to ignore the authentic polemic of
Jesus against the Pharisees on the pretext that this was merely an
invention of the Church in its battle against Judaism. There were
even some Christian scholars who believed so.

The process of Jewish identification with the concept "Pharisees" occurred in two stages:

a) In the Middle Ages, when the Karaite movement arose
inside Judaism and rejected the Oral Law, the Karaites identified
with the ancient Sadducees. This was the time when the Rabbis
began to identify with the Pharisees, without realizing that the
word "Pharisees" never appears in the Talmudic sources as a
general designation of the Sages (except when used by their
opponents).

b) When the Christians began to apply the words of Jesus
against the Pharisees as directed against Rabbinic Judaism in
general. As an act of self-defense, the Jews began to identify the
concept of "Pharisees" with the Sages.

In the past, the word "Pharisees" was used as a title of abuse
for people who kept themselves apart from all the rest. One can

note here a blessing which once existed in the <u>Jewish Silent Prayer</u> (the *Amidah*) instead of the present Blessing against Heretics, and which was directed against those who separated themselves from the main body of the nation, designating them as "Pharisees" (*Tosephta, Berakhot*, 3:25). There is therefore in the whole of Talmudic literature not a single Sage designated as a Pharisee, and the word appears only in some isolated usages – in the case of the extension of purification rituals, one finds references to a "Pharisee" in matters of gonorrhea (one who is more stringent with himself than are most people when being purified from gonorrhea), and similar usages. We do find in Talmudic literature that the designation "Pharisees" was used by the enemies of the Sages in disputes with them. For example, in disputations between the Sages and the Sadducees, the Sadducees addressed the Sages as "Pharisees." The Talmud, on the other hand, speaks of the "Sanhedrin of Israel" (*Megillat Taanit*), and the Pharisees used to call themselves "Israel" or "the Sages of Israel." <u>They were not people who had withdrawn from the ways of the people, but they were Israel itself, and therein lay their strength.</u>

Another connotation of the term "Pharisees" is to be found where the Sages themselves speak of their own negative traits. They speak, for example, of the Seven Plagues of the Pharisees (*Jer. Berakhot* 9, 14b). One should point out, though, that in Jewish literature written in Greek, the limitation on the use of "Pharisees" has been removed, and Josephus can thus define himself as a Pharisee. The same applied to Paul, who can designate himself as a Pharisee without any negative connotation (Philippians 3:5). But as we have noted, the use of the word "Pharisee" is limited, and Josephus and Paul proclaim themselves as Pharisees in writings which are chiefly meant for external consumption. In Acts 5:34 Rabban Gamaliel the Elder is described as a Pharisee.

In the rabbinic literature, there is another use of the word "Pharisee," being used as the designation of sinister groups, circles of people who had separated themselves from Judaism or had abandoned it. The term also received another negative connotation, as found in the Talmud: referring to flatterers and dissemblers. The word "dissembler," which is the equivalent of the word "hypocrite" in Christian parlance, has its origin in the Greek version of the New Testament. The Hebrew for "dissembler," *zavu'a*, is derived from the admonition of the Hasmonean King Alexander Jannaeus to his wife, exhorting her not to fear either the Pharisees or those who were not Pharisees, but to fear only the *zevu'im* (the "colored ones"), who "act like Zimri and await the reward of Phineas" (*Bab. Sotah* 22).

This expression is reminiscent of one point in Jesus' polemic against the Pharisees, where Jesus compared them to sepulchres which are whitewashed outside but are full of maggots inside. We find this simile in Matthew 23:27–28. Another passage in the same chapter (Matthew 23:4) helps us understand another Talmudic reference. According to this passage in Matthew, Jesus claimed that the Pharisees laid heavy burdens on other men's shoulders, but did not move them with even one of their fingers.

The Jerusalem Talmud tells us of one of the negative characters among the Pharisees, a person who was called the Shechemite Pharisee. The Jerusalem Talmud explains he was a citizen of Shechem (Nablus today), and the Babylonian Talmud adds that he used to follow the practices of the Shechemites. The people of Shechem converted to Judaism only as far as outward appearances were concerned, as we are told in the story of Jacob and his sons in Genesis 33–34. The Jerusalem Talmud (*Berakhot*) says: "He lays the burden of the commandments on the shoulder" (*shechem* means "shoulder" in Hebrew). The commentators explain that he puts the commandments on his shoulders in order to show them to others. But if one puts something on one's shoulder, it is obvious that another has to help him to bear it. The late Professor Eduard Yechezkel Kutscher confirmed my own suggestion that one could take the words "lay the burden" to mean "lay the burden of the commandments on *other people's* shoulders."

It is no accident that this kind of Pharisee appears as the first in the list of seven kinds of Pharisees in the Talmud. In Jesus' speech in Matthew, this kind of Pharisee also appears at the beginning of his polemic against the Pharisees. It appears, then, that in the world of the Sages there were negative characters whose words did not correspond to their deeds. These were the dissemblers. A dissembling Pharisee would assume that if a man was drowning his rescuer had to take off his phylacteries before jumping in to save him; or that it was better to look up to heaven and stumble and fall rather than look at a woman; and the favorite saying of such a one would be: "Give me a commandment, and I will perform it."

The strictures of the Sages against this negative type of Pharisee were identical with those of Jesus against the Pharisees. Jesus said of them that they made broad their phylacteries and loved the chief seats in the synagogues in order to be seen and to be called Rabbi. Likewise, as we have mentioned, Jesus compared the Pharisees to sepulchres which are whitewashed on the outside but full of maggots inside. In Matthew 23, Jesus stated seven times "woe unto you... Pharisees." In the Talmud seven types of Pharisees are listed, five of them hypocrites.

Jesus did, however, also have positive things to say about the Pharisees. He was aware that in the world of the Pharisees there was a certain hypocrisy, but at the same time, he was also aware of the positive aspects of the Pharisees; in other words, there was an intentional ambiguity in his use of the word "Pharisees." He also said: "The scribes and the Pharisees sit in Moses' seat: All therefore whatsoever they bid you observe, that observe and do; but do not you after their works: for they say, and do not" (Matthew 23:2–3). Here he was making a clear distinction between the negative types of Pharisees and the rest of the Pharisees; he spoke of the Pharisees in general, but inserted into his speech the polemic we find in the Talmudic sources against the negative kinds of Pharisees.

Jesus emphasized that the ways of the Sages should guide his disciples, since the Sages, as he stated, sat on the seat of Moses, and their rulings were binding on him and his disciples. Jesus also required of his disciples that their righteousness should exceed that of the Pharisees (Matthew 5:20). He saw in the Pharisees the heirs of Moses and therefore the true interpreters of the Torah; but he also criticized them for not doing what they said.

This poses the question: How should we define the Pharisees in terms of their social position? They are called hypocrites by Jesus, by the Essenes, and in Talmudic literature. It is difficult to ascertain who were the people in the world of the Sages who drove such different men as Jesus, the Sadducee King Jannaeus, and the Essenes, into seeking or discovering in the Pharisaic world men who were hypocrites. An answer proposed by the late Professor Yadin was that those – such as the Essenes and in some areas the Sadducees – who took a stringent line in matters of the Law saw the more lenient approach of the Rabbinic Jews as hypocrisy. I cannot share this view.

During the period of crystallization of the world of the Sages, which went on until the renewal in Jamnia, when the belief in the application of the commandments to all areas of life and all strata of the population had not yet been commonly accepted, there must have been people who accepted the more stringent rulings only outwardly; who took the more stringent line only to impress others, perhaps including also themselves. It is obvious that such people could be found especially among those who took the more stringent line consistently – that is, the School of Shammai. It is possible that such people disappeared after the destruction of the Temple and the victory of the School of Hillel over the School of Shammai, when the keeping of the commandments in all areas of life became perfectly natural. This is why, as time went on, the more lenient rulings of the School of Hillel were accepted.

It is interesting to note that in all that is said against Rabbinic Judaism in the works of the Church Fathers, there is not a single accusation of hypocrisy levelled against the Sages. By that time, it appears, this type of hypocrisy no longer existed – either because the Pharisaic approach had already become common property, or because of the victory of the School of Hillel.

V.

Jesus and Second Temple Pietism

JESUS WAS CLOSE TO THE WORLD OF THE HASSIDIM (THE "Pious"), who were in their turn close to the world of the Sages, but were not entirely identical with them.

Professor Shmuel Safrai, who has done much work investigating these groups of the Pious, distinguishes between the Pious we know from the First Book of Maccabees, who were some kind of militant group who joined Mattathias the Hasmonean, and the later ones, to whom Jesus was related.

The Pious of the Hasmonean period were men of war, and it appears that they were especially strict in matters of ritual purification. At that time there was a controversy as to whether these purification laws were binding on the whole of Israel, or whether each individual could make up his mind whether to accept them or not. The Pious to whom Jesus belonged were not scrupulous in matters of purification. In general, they were opposed to the emphasis put on the study of the Torah as a supreme value, and instead emphasized the importance of good deeds. One should mention, as an example, Honi the Circle-Drawer, who was killed in 62 B.C.E. Honi drew a circle and prayed for rain, and this brought about a clash between him and Simeon ben Shetah, who at the time represented the Sages' establishment. One should also mention Rabbi Hanina ben Dosa, who lived just before and after the destruction of the Temple and was close to Rabban Yohanan ben Zakkai. According to Rabbi Hanina, wisdom is not on a par with good deeds (*Avot* 3:12).

These Pious opposed the growing tendency towards intellectualism. Indeed, most of the Sages accepted the view of the Pious, that "not learning but doing is the chief thing" as stated by Rabbi Simeon ben Gamaliel (*Avot* 1:17). The tension between good deeds and intellectualism continued until 120 C.E., when the Sages concluded, after a long debate among themselves, that the study of the Torah takes precedence, since it leads one to action. Jesus always emphasized the importance of action. He commanded his disciples to act according to the rulings of the Pharisees, and frequently spoke of doing the will of his Father in Heaven. Study always took second place with Jesus, although he was far more learned than most people of his social position, and certainly more learned than Paul, although Paul studied in Jerusalem.

The Pious were regarded as sons of God. When Honi the Circle-Drawer had brought about rain, Simeon ben Shetah said to him: "Were you not Honi, I would have had you excommunicated... but what can I do to you, who coax the Almighty to do your will, like a son who coaxes his father to do his will?" (*Bab. Taanit* 23a). And when Rabban Yohanan ben Zakkai asked Rabbi Hanina ben Dosa to pray for him, he explained that he himself could not pray, since he stood before the Blessed One as a dignitary, while Rabbi Hanina stood before Him as His familiar servant (*Bab. Berakhot* 34b).

When the world was short of rain, the Sages used to send for a Pious man called Yohanan the Withdrawn. They would send children, who would grasp at the edge of his garment and implore him: "Father, father, bring us rain." The Pious man would then say: "Master of the Universe, do it for the sake of those who do not discern between a father who brings rain and a father who does not bring rain" (*Bab. Taanit* 23b). Long ago scholars noticed the similarity between this story and Jesus' usual address to God, "Father!" They noted the parallel between the feeling of familiarity with God among the Pious and Jesus' special familiarity with his Father in Heaven. Jesus felt that he was a son of God. The Sages, too, recognized the special familiar relation of the Pious to God, a relation which originated in their extraordinary deeds.

It is no accident that a divine voice referred to Rabbi Hanina ben Dosa as "Hanina my son." This enables us to understand Jesus as one of those Pious. Jesus' anti-intellectualism was an exact counterpart of the anti-intellectualism of the Pious. Jesus was most probably one of them.

Of crucial importance is the designation of the Pious as "men of action." This last word, "action," is in many cases contrasted with the study of the Torah and its exegesis, but in our case it connotes something more extreme. The Pious did not interrupt their prayers even when they were in danger of their lives. It was their belief that it was not the snake that killed, but sin, and there was no reason, therefore, to stop praying just because a snake might be coiled about one's leg. Their contemporaries also believed that the Pious could perform supernatural acts, such as bringing rain and healing through their prayers. Jesus, the popular preacher, who regarded himself as close to God – as his ally or son – and who was even capable of healing the sick, clearly falls within the framework of the Pious of that period.

There is another point of similarity between Jesus and the Pious. Although the Pious were strict in what they demanded of themselves – just as Jesus required of his disciples that their righteousness should exceed that of the scribes and Pharisees – they had an appeal to wide strata of the population. They even showed sympathy toward the publicans, who were usually excluded from society. Jesus too had this tendency to draw toward him society's rejects, including sinners and publicans.

The outlook of these Pious has been preserved even in Talmudic literature. The Pious were strict on moral issues and lenient in the more ritual and institutional matters of Jewish Law – for example, in purification laws. So was Jesus. This explains why Jesus had sympathy with the strict rulings of the School of Shammai whenever they were concerned with the fear of sin. It appears

A Herodian era stone carving in Greek, which indicates that entrance is forbidden to the Temple.

that Jesus' view here paralleled that of the Pious. It is only for a lack of information on the rulings of the Pious that we cannot describe with accuracy their peculiar fusion of the strictness of the School of Shammai and the School of Hillel's love of one's fellow man. The extensive literature which has reached us concerning them is close in its spirit to Jesus' ways. It is perhaps in those parts of Talmudic literature which deal with good manners (*Derekh Eretz*, originally ethics) that one can detect relics of the rulings of the Pious. It is also possible that the view which regards the most minor commandment as equal to the greatest, which we find in the writings of the Sages, belongs precisely to the doctrine of the Pious, one of whose representatives was Jesus. This may explain the moderate suspicions against Jesus which arose in the world of the Sages: they were capable of suspecting other Pious men just as well.

VI.

Jesus Between the World of Rabbinic Judaism and the World of the Essenes

THE DEAD SEA SCROLLS HAVE DISCLOSED A WHOLE WORLD OF Judaism, the world of the Essenes – the Sons of Light – who dwelled in the wilderness of Judea, separated themselves from the rest of Israel, and developed their own peculiar religious and social institutions. Our sources concerning them are ancient writers, especially Josephus and Philo, and their own writings. From the newly discovered Scrolls one is now able to write a commentary on Josephus' passages which deal with the Essenes.

Jesus grew up in a home which was probably steeped in learning, and he probably studied with men who were close to the world of the Sages. He met the Essenes through John the Baptist, but he had known them as "the Sons of Light," and this is how he referred to them. In Chapter 16 of the Gospel of Luke, he showed an attitude of both respect and contempt toward these Sons of Light, who made themselves no friends of the mammon of unrighteousness – that is, those people who were called the Sons of Light secluded themselves from the rest of Israel and rejected any financial undertakings with those who did not belong to their group. Jesus regarded the men of the world as wiser than the Sons of Light, and there is no doubt that the "Sons of Light" here is a reference to the Essenes.

By and large, Jesus, like the large majority of Israel, tended toward the world of the Sages. At the same time, there was also some contact between him and the Essenes, as emerges from the Scrolls. Jesus preached "Thou shalt love thy neighbor as thyself," and required a man to return love even to his enemy. It would have suited Jesus' doctrine better if he had distanced himself from the world of the Essenes, who saw in hatred towards the Sons of Darkness – those who did not belong to the sect – a supreme religious obligation. Jesus in no way accepted the sect's world-view, but he learned from it.

The Essenes secluded themselves from the world around them. They shared all their money – a rare occurrence in the Jewish world. They had no money and no slaves. Moreover, as we learn from the Scrolls, they valued poverty as a religious value and called themselves "the paupers of Your redemption." For the Essenes, that was an honorary title of the sect. They sensed the danger inherent in riches, which can pull a man away from God. It is true that we sometimes find this positive approach to poverty even among the Sages; but in general, the Sages regard poverty as something which should be relieved, and wish there were no poor men. Here we find a difference in principle between the Sages and the Essenes. The Essenes were dissenters and righteous, as they were devoid of the desire for money.

In one of his famous expressions, Jesus took both the side of the Sages and the side of the Essenes. He said that "No man can serve two masters... Ye cannot serve God and mammon" (Matthew 6:24; Luke 16:13). The Sages described man as a servant of two masters – his instincts and his Creator. Jesus grafted on the Essene element to the saying of the Sages, speaking of the contrast between God and mammon as a duality between poverty and property, just as is found in the Essene documents.

In the sayings of Jesus, we find the expression "the poor in spirit" – that is, poor men who have received the gift of the holy spirit. The expression appears in a renowned poetic passage, beginning with three famous Beatitudes: "Blessed are the poor in spirit, for theirs is the kingdom of heaven; Blessed are they that mourn for they shall be comforted; Blessed are the meek, for they shall inherit the earth" (Matthew 5:3–5). This passage and what follows have a parallel in the Thanksgiving Hymns of the Dead Sea Sect, and one can point out the literary connections between one particular passage of the Essene Hymns (18:14–15) and the words of Jesus. There, too, we find the poor in spirit, the meek and the mourners together. From the passage in the Scrolls and from the New Testament it appears that Jesus, just as much as the Essenes, regarded it as his duty to fulfill that which was written in Isaiah, "the Lord hath anointed me to preach good tidings to the meek" (cf. also Luke 4:16–20).

In Matthew 11:25–30, we have a whole such Thanksgiving Hymn preserved, written in the style of the Essene Hymns: "I thank Thee, O Father, Lord of heaven and earth, because Thou hast hid these things from the wise and the prudent, and hast revealed them unto the simple ones..." The opening words, "I thank Thee," appears in most of the Essene Thanksgiving Hymns. The idea that the deepest truth is closed to certain people also belongs to the world of the Essenes. Even the word "simple," hinting as it does to opposition toward the intellectualism of "the wise and the prudent," comes from the world of the Essenes, and to some extent from that of the Pious.

There was, however, a difference between Jesus and the Essenes. What was common to them were certain social doctrines. But Jesus accepted the world of the Sages, and even when he adopted certain Essene doctrines, he did not observe them with the extreme strictness of the Essenes themselves. It is obvious that he did not accept the attitude which called for seclusion from the world or from the seat of the unrighteous; on the contrary, he addressed himself to the entire world, with its sinners.

The Essenes laid stress on poverty as a religious value, as followed from their extreme attitude to the value of righteousness. They regarded themselves as the chosen ones of righteousness, and the rest of the people they regarded, at best, as righteous in the future. Jesus and the School of Hillel did not stress the issue of righteousness to such an extreme. Jesus spoke not of justice, but of love, and so did the Sages. The Essenes probably regarded Jesus as a dangerous man, a man who could say "Blessed are the poor in spirit, for theirs is the kingdom of heaven," and at the same time could converse with publicans and prostitutes.

The essential difference between the world of Jesus and that of the Essenes arose not only from Jesus' unique personality, but also from his identification with the traditions of the Pious and the Sages. Jesus agreed with the Essenes about the social principle of the value of poverty; but he could not accept the extreme dualism which called for a separation between the community of the righteous and the world of sin. At the same time, we can learn from the Scrolls to what an extent a fusion between the dissenting Essenes and the Pious was still possible in those days. Jesus stood at the point of coincidence between them, but his main tendency was toward the Pious, who constituted something of a left wing in the world of the Sages. We have evidence for this peculiar *rapprochement* between the dissenting party of the Essenes and the party of the Pious both in Essene literature and in the literature of the Sages.

Two documents related to the Dead Sea Scrolls have been preserved in the ancient Christian literature: One is the important Greek work, *The Testament of the Patriarchs*, which is also extant in Armenian translation. In the Greek work, related to the Dead Sea Sect, the speakers are the twelve sons of Jacob, who hand down their doctrines to their families before their deaths. We find here close ties with the world of the Essenes in, for example, the dualism of good and evil and the emergence of Belial. On the other hand, this work lays great value on one's attitude towards one's fellow man. Whereas the Essene documents indicate a religious hatred toward the evil world, the *Testaments of the Patriarchs* portray love even toward the wicked. One should triumph over evil by doing good to the wicked, thus causing them to mend their ways.

It is rather in this composition than in the Scrolls that we find a broad similarity to Jesus' Beatitudes. Here, and in the other source, *The Treatise of the Two Ways* (a part of the early Christian *Doctrine of the Apostles*) we also find Jesus' favorite combination of "Thou shalt love the Lord thy God" with "Thou shalt love thy neighbor as thyself." This doctrine was acceptable to the circles which were close to the dissenting Essenes, but which did not wish to become a separatist sect or to preach institutional hatred.

Among the Sages too, we can find parallels to Jesus' doctrines. In the two treatises on manners (*Derekh Eretz*), and especially in *Derekh Eretz Zuta*, we encounter the issue of the equality between a minor and a major commandment. The very expression "*Derekh Eretz*" – "the way of the world" – is reminiscent of the two ways (*derakhim*) of which the Essenes often speak – the way of good and the way of evil. These are described in the other work of the dissenting Essenes – *The Treatise on the Two Ways*.

We are here, apparently, at the point where two worlds coincide. At the point where they coincide, it is difficult to discern the humane dissenting Essene from the Pious, who lives in a state of tension toward the Sages. It is exactly at this point that Jesus stands, and it is therefore true that both the literature of the dissenting Essenes and that of the Sages illuminate the sayings of Jesus in the Gospels.

VII.

The Influence of John the Baptist on Jesus

ONE OF THE MOST IMPORTANT FIGURES IN THE HISTORY OF
Christianity is John the Baptist. John was a solitary, who literally
took upon himself the task pointed out by Isaiah: "In the wilderness prepare ye the way of the Lord, make straight in the desert a
highway for our God." He sat near the Jordan and baptized people
who came to him. Thus he gave Christianity the sacrament of
baptism, which to this day signifies adherence to the Christian
community. Jesus himself did not baptize, but it appears that
following the entrance of the adherents of John the Baptist into the
Christian community, the Christians adopted this ritual. This in-
fluential man, who was loved by the Jewish people, was executed
by Herod Antipas.

Our sources concerning John the Baptist are the New Testament and the words of Josephus (*Antiquities* XVIII, 116–119).
Josephus' interpretation of the significance of John's baptism is
almost identical to the theology of baptism in the Dead Sea Scrolls.
It appears that there was indeed an affinity between John the
Baptist and the Essenes, and scholars assume that John was once a
member of the Essene sect and left the sect for ideological reasons.

Baptism – both for John the Baptist and for the Essenes – had the same significance as the Jewish ritual of immersion in a *mikveh* (a special pool of rain water used for purification purposes). The Essenes, and John following them, adopted the idea that immersion purified the body, but they believed that a person's body was defiled not only through contact with objects which were ritually unclean, but also through sin. When someone sinned his body was defiled, and therefore a man who had not repented before his immersion would not become pure. While the immersion might purify the body, the body would immediately be defiled again through the person's sin.

This approach was adopted by John the Baptist. Numerous people flocked to him, since he did not require them to abandon their usual way of life, to give away their property to a communal fund, or to form a separate sect. They simply hoped to redeem their souls through confession and immersion. There were even some who believed mistakenly that immersion itself would purify them from their sins. These people did not grasp the idea that repentance purified a man from sin and water only purified the body.

Both the Gospels and Josephus relate the precautions imparted by John the Baptist to people about to be immersed. Immersion was not intended as a forgiveness of sins, but merely as a purification for the body, after the soul had been purified by deeds of righteousness and by repentance.

John had to fight against the conception of immersion as a miracle, which acted in itself as a purification from sin. This mistaken conception was later adopted by the Christians, and baptism was turned into a sacrament.

What the people were seeking was the forgiveness of sins, and John caused a misapprehension, albeit through the best intentions. He believed that the Essenes had made a mistake in dividing Israel through the creation of a separate sect. He therefore offered all members of Israel the possibility of accepting the rite of immersion without changing their social status.

In the light of all this, we can understand John's answer to those who approached him (Luke 3:10–14), where he permitted them to continue in their occupations. Soldiers remained soldiers and publicans remained publicans. Among the Essenes, publicans were regarded as corrupt because of their indecent gains, and soldiers were considered as the accomplices of the Sons of Darkness. John the Baptist brought about a reform out of a feeling of love for Israel.

For a broader understanding of the position of John the Baptist, we should be familiar with the Essene elements in Jesus' doctrines. For example, John required, instead of community of property within the sect, the sharing of one's property with the poor. So did Jesus. As he said: "If any man will... take away thy coat, let him have thy cloak also" (Matthew 5:40). On this issue John the Baptist modified the stricter Essene ruling, and it appears that Jesus adopted this lenient approach in order to appeal to the whole of Israel.

Let us take another example. Josephus (*Wars* 2:125) tells us that messengers of the Essenes carried no provisions with them since wherever they went the Essene groups would have stores and would supply all their needs. Jesus, too, advised the pupils whom he sent out to spread the gospel of the Kingdom of Heaven not to take any provisions; but unlike the Essenes, he told his apostles that the people whose towns they would enter would provide them, since the workman is worthy of his meat (Matthew 10:9–14). One can assume once again that Jesus adopted this approach, which does not accept a full community of property, from John the Baptist.

Of John's attitude we can also learn from the words of Jesus himself. We should stress that Jesus did, indeed, know the Essenes, but the Essene elements which we find, such as a positive attitude toward poverty, the concepts of the "poor in spirit" and of the simple ones, Jesus' opposition to wealth and his criticism of the Sages' intellectualism – all these he learned from John the Baptist. And John, according to the testimony of Josephus and of the New Testament, was accepted by the whole of Israel as a holy man and a prophet. The people believed that John the Baptist was the Prophet Elijah who had ascended to heaven in a storm.

Even after John's execution, the people still believed that he had not died but had come back to life. Just as Elijah had been turned into a immortal figure, so had John the Baptist. When he was executed on the orders of Herod Antipas, the belief that he had come back to life was born (Matthew 14:1–2; 16:14). It is reasonable to assume that the belief in the resurrection of John the Baptist also influenced the belief in Jesus' resurrection, since Jesus' disciples included former disciples of John.

According to the Gospel of Luke, Jesus came to John the Baptist, was immersed by him, and probably lived for a while in his company until he left him. According to Mark and Matthew, however, Jesus began to preach his gospels only after John the Baptist had been imprisoned. In any case, the fact is that Jesus separated himself from John the Baptist and founded a community of his own. Jesus praised John the Baptist, on the one hand, and differed from him, on the other, and it appears that there were some differences between them.

When John the Baptist sent messengers to Jesus to inquire if he was the Messiah, Jesus hinted to him of his Messiahship with the words: "And blessed is he, whosoever shall not stumble in me" (Matthew 11:6).

But it was not a mere personal feud which made Jesus abandon John, but also a difference in outlook. John's roots were in the world of the Essenes. Like the Essenes, he regarded his own generation as the last one. People who saw in him the Prophet Elijah regarded him as the divine messenger arriving before the Day of the Lord. Jesus, on the other hand, had his roots in the world of the Sages. He had a unique historical conscience, and saw in his generation not the generation of the end of days, but the first movement in which the Kingdom of Heaven was taking shape. This ideological difference between them made Jesus take exception to John the Baptist. He saw in him the great prophet, but he also claimed that "he that is least in the Kingdom of Heaven is greater than he" (Matthew 11:11).

VIII.

Jesus and the Kingdom of Heaven

UNTIL RECENTLY, EVEN JEWISH SCHOLARS ACCEPTED WITHOUT hesitation the Christian view that Jesus regarded himself as the Messiah. In recent years, even Christian scholars have begun to doubt this assumption. *False*

Jesus did not call the Messiah by his name, but spoke of him as *Bar Enash* (Son of Man). He spoke of a man who was to come, but he never stated explicitly that he himself was that man. It appears that sometimes Jesus regarded himself as the Messiah or came to the conclusion that he might be the Messiah. During the period of the Second Temple there were other people who asked themselves whether they were the Messiah.

Jesus regarded his relationship with God as that of a son to his father. Here, too, he was hardly unique. The Pious and saints of that period felt especially close to God and defined their relation to Him as that of sons to a father. But Jesus, under the influence of the Essenes and through the example of their prophets, saw himself also as a revealer of divine secrets. He gave thanks to his God with the words "I thank thee, O Father, Lord of heaven and earth, because thou hast hid these things from the wise and prudent, and hast revealed them unto the simple ones." He continued and stated that just as among men "no man knows the Son, but the Father;

neither knows any man the Father, but the Son, and he to whomever the Son will reveal Him" (Matthew 11:25;27), so was this true in relation to himself. This Thanksgiving Hymn was intentionally phrased by Jesus in the style of the Qumran Thanksgiving Hymns.

Jesus regarded himself as a son who revealed the secrets of his Father in Heaven, and spoke of the Almighty as "Father." This attitude was at the root of both the development of Christian theology and the story of Jesus' birth without an earthly father.

In Jesus' own sayings, we do not find the word "redemption" in its religious, eschatological sense; but Jesus did use the expression "the Kingdom of Heaven." This expression, which was current in many circles, combined in Matthew 5:3 the Essene attitude of respect for poverty with the idea of the Kingdom of Heaven. Jesus said: "Blessed are the poor in spirit, for theirs is the kingdom of heaven." Rabban Yohanan ben Zakkai, a contemporary of Jesus, also used the expression "the Kingdom of Heaven." From him and from other sources it appears that this expression, "the Kingdom of Heaven," is a well-defined concept which was employed in the polemics against the Zealots, who advocated a war against Rome.

The Zealots believed that the acceptance of Roman rule as an accomplished fact, in theory or in practice, was an unforgivable sin on the part of the Jewish people. They espoused the tradition going back to the Prophet Samuel that God was Israel's only king, and that it was unlawful for the people of Israel to subject themselves to the rule of a king, and all the more so to the rule of a foreign king. Both the Zealots and the Essenes saw the Kingdom of Heaven as an event which was to occur at some future time (although the Essenes did not use the term itself). Jose the Galilean said about the verse from Moses' Song on the Red Sea, "The Lord *shall reign* for ever and ever" (Exodus 16:18), that it was regrettable that Moses had put it that way, for, had he said "The Lord *has reigned* for ever and ever," the Kingdom of Heaven would have come about immediately (see *Mekhilta* on this verse).

This was the attitude of the Sages of the School of Hillel. In their opinion, what mattered was not whether one accepted Roman rule or rejected it; for the Kingdom of Heaven could come about at any time, once the people repented and took upon themselves the yoke of the Kingdom of Heaven – and once that happened, no nation or tongue would hold sway over them. Only then would God fulfill his promise to rule over Israel. No rebellion against Rome would help, but the kingdom of Rome would vanish once the people had taken upon themselves the yoke of the Kingdom of Heaven.

The Sages believed that even when a man recites "Hear O Israel," he is taking upon himself the Kingdom of Heaven and is living under it. The Kingdom of Heaven existed there and then, and was in no way conditioned by a rebellion against Rome, but only by the purity of the people of Israel. Jesus employed this term, "the Kingdom of Heaven," exactly in this sense. For him, too, the Kingdom of Heaven already existed, and one needed to work for its complete realization. *future*

In Jesus' view, John the Baptist had also fulfilled a task in the process of the realization of the Kingdom of Heaven. Jesus said that "All the prophets ... prophesied until John" (Matthew 11:13). In other words, John the Baptist was the man who had begun the process of realization of the Kingdom of Heaven, and Jesus had then brought it to fulfillment through the dissemination of his ideas and the foundation of his movement.

It thus appears that Jesus was no Zealot, but was close to the moderate circles of the School of Hillel. Jesus developed the idea of the Kingdom of Heaven in a personal manner. He believed that the Kingdom of Heaven would spread and be realized if he succeeded in developing around him a movement which would bring people to repent, and thus avoid the threat of destruction of the Second Temple. He followed here in the steps of prophets like Jeremiah, and offered the people a way of life which was the opposite of that of the Zealots, and was also somewhat different from that of the Sages. He placed himself at the center of a movement which served as an instrument for disseminating the Kingdom of Heaven, which would solve the problems of the people of Israel. This movement was itself, as it were, the realization of

Jesus crucified, from a 17th century Ethiopian manuscript.

◀ *Eighth Station of the Cross – Via Dolorosa, Jerusalem.*

the Kingdom of Heaven.

Jesus regarded the Kingdom of Heaven as taking shape around him and together with him. Later on, Christianity was influenced by this idea, but in a somewhat distorted manner, and identified the idea of the Kingdom of Heaven with the community itself – the Christian Church – or with redemption after death.

Jesus thus stood at the center of a movement which was to bring about, step by step, the realization of the Kingdom of Heaven on earth. It was in accordance with this idea that he explained the miracles, the signs and the healing he brought about for the people. Miracles, in Jesus' view, were not isolated phenomena, but were evidence that the Devil had already fallen, and that they were beholding the realization of the Kingdom of Heaven on earth.

There is a difference between the attitude of the Sages and Jesus' approach. The Sages believed that the Kingdom of Heaven had always existed and had only to be brought to fulfillment, but they gave no date for that fulfillment. Jesus believed that the process of realization of the Kingdom of Heaven had already begun by the work of John the Baptist, who had broken forth into the Kingdom of Heaven although he had not quite entered it himself. It is reasonable to assume that at times Jesus thought that he was not only at the center of this process, but that he was himself the Messiah, who was bringing the Kingdom of Heaven upon Israel.

IX.

The Concept of the Messiah

THE NEW TESTAMENT REFLECTS THE VARIOUS SHADES OF JEWISH messianic belief in the period of the Second Temple. Beside the sayings of Jesus himself, it reflects other streams in Judaism, with different conceptions of redemption and of the image of the Messiah.

The image of the Messiah in Judaism is usually less important than the idea of redemption as one expects it to occur. The Messiah is the person who is to fulfill this redemption. One should note here that under the influence of Maimonides, and later, under the influence of Jewish rationalism and because of the opposition to Christianity, many important aspects of the belief in the Messiah and in redemption were not properly investigated.

Under the influence of Maimonides, Judaism has endeavored to minimize the importance of Messianic beliefs. Maimonides quotes the Babylonian Talmud to the effect that even in the days of the Messiah the world will continue in its usual ways, except that Israel will no longer be subservient to alien kingdoms. The Sages did, indeed, attempt to strengthen the Messianic hope, and they succeeded in doing this. But they objected to the increasingly superhuman aspects of this hope. Nevertheless, there are echoes, even in their writings, of such Messianic conceptions.

In Jewish apocryphal literature and in medieval Jewish literature we find many different conceptions of the figure of the Messiah. The most moderate view is that in the days of the Messiah Israel's servitude to alien kingdoms will come to an end. In the Midrashic literature, the ways of the Messiah acquire a dimension which is beyond everyday life and passes human understanding. In Jewish prayers, the word Messiah does not appear, and the expressions used are such as "the Branch of David."

Jesus does not speak of the Messiah as such. He uses an expression also found in the seventh chapter of the Book of Daniel: Son of Man, or *Bar Enash*. This expression is found not only in the New Testament, but also in the book of Daniel, in the Jewish Apocrypha, and especially in a passage of the Book of Enoch which has been preserved in full in an Ethiopian translation (Chaps. 37–71).

The image of this *Bar Enash* is fascinating and unique. It is the figure of an almost superhuman judge, who is to sit on the throne of God and to separate the righteous from the wicked. He is to deliver the righteous to everlasting life and the wicked to everlasting punishment.

There are hints of *Bar Enash* even in the sayings of the Sages. When Rabbi Akiva hinted at this figure, the other Sages rejected his view and advised him to go and occupy himself with the study of the Law, since the Messiah will be human, not an angel.

The expression "Son of Man" (Hebrew: *Ben Adam*) connects this figure with Adam, the first man. In one of the Jewish Apocrypha (*The Testament of Abraham*), this expression is interpreted literally as the son of the Biblical Adam and is identified with Abel, the brother of Cain, who will be the judge at the end of days. This connection between the Messiah and the Biblical Adam can also be found in the literature of the Sages: according to Reish Lakish, the spirit of the Messiah is identical with the breath of life which God breathed into Adam's nostrils. It is identified, on the one hand, with the spirit of God which moved upon the face of the waters, and on the other hand, with the spirit of God mentioned in Isaiah 11:2, which God will instill within the Messiah.

A section of the Temple *Scrolls. This particular scroll enumerates the practices of the Dead Sea sect.*

In the writings of Paul, it appears that the spirit upon the waters is the spirit of Adam and also the spirit of the Messiah. The connection between the Messiah and Adam was accepted by Christianity, and brought about the further connection between Original Sin, the First Man, and the Last Man, who is Jesus the Christ. The Last Man atones for the sin of the First Man — an idea which later became one of the principles of Christian belief.

There are many exalted things said about the Messiah in Jewish literature, and the sublime conceptions of Christ the Messiah in the New Testament are, in most cases, not the direct result of Christian belief, but adaptations and modifications of Jewish beliefs which were current in certain circles. Thus, in the Epistle to the Hebrews, we are told that the Messiah is greater than the Patriarchs, and especially Abraham; that he is greater than Moses and more sublime than the Archangels. This conception, which appears at first sight to be typically Christian, can be found in *Midrash Tanhuma*, and hints of it can be detected in even earlier Rabbinic literature, the literature of the Tannaim (the early Talmudic Sages in Palestine).

Since Jesus was regarded as Messiah and Son of God and was literally identified with God, the New Testament has preserved expressions and views current in Judaism at the time of Jesus and ascribed to him. Thus we can reconstruct some chapters in the history of Jewish faith at the time, with its various sects and streams.

This applies not only to Jesus and his conception of himself, but especially to the literature of the New Testament, the Epistles of Paul and other Epistles. Christianity brought about a combination of the sublime view of the Messiah as someone who was already present at the hour of creation, as we are told in the Book of Enoch, and the Jewish motif of atonement for the sins of Israel through the martyrdom of the saints. This conception, which is in no way central to Judaism, resembles the popular idea that "they died to bequeath us life." Marginal to this conception, we have the mythological idea that the death of those who have sacrificed themselves for our sake atones for our sins just as a proper sacrifice.

Since the age of the Hasmoneans, Jews had believed that the saints who died to sanctify the name of God atoned for the sins of Israel. The story of the mother and her seven sons in the Second Book of Maccabees acquires a greater significance in the Fourth Book of Maccabees, where their death is seen as an atoning sacrifice. In another Jewish source, *Midrash Sifre*, the idea is expressed that the killing of the Children of Israel by the Gentiles atones for the former's sins (*Sifre* to Deut. 32:43).

It is reasonable to assume that during the Roman period this idea was applied not only to Jesus, but also to all those who were executed by the authorities. Even Jews who did not accept Christianity evidently believed that Jesus, like the other martyrs of the Roman authorities, had atoned for the sins of Israel.

It appears that this mythological conception was current in those days. It was later connected to the Christian belief that Jesus was the Messiah in the sublime form of *Bar Enash*, and thus the sublime Jewish conceptions of the Messiah, which did not occupy a very central position in the world of the Sages, were amalgamated with the idea of atonement through Jesus, which became in Christianity the idea that there is no atonement except through Jesus. Christians do not believe – as Jews have always done – that their martyrs atone for their sins; the atonement for sins through the blood of Jesus is reserved only for the Son of God, for Jesus himself.

To sum up: the celestial biography found in the New Testament consists entirely of Jewish motifs: Jesus the Messiah had existed before the creation of the world; he entered the world, or even created it; he became flesh – this is an innovation – and then brought about redemption; he is the Messiah – *Bar Enash*, the Last Adam; and he atones for sins just like those who had atoned for the sins of Israel and then comes back to life.

The term "Christos," which is a Greek translation of the Hebrew "Messiah," already appears in the Septuagint, and thereafter in the New Testament. When the Christians abandoned Judaism, they no longer understood the word "Christian," and explained it as yet another epithet of Jesus. They did not usually understand this concept of the Messiah as the savior of Israel; but perhaps just because of this change in the structure of Christian belief in the Messiah the New Testament has preserved for us Jewish conceptions from the period of the Second Temple.

X.

The Midrash and the New Testament

THE MIDRASH ORIGINATED IN A PERIOD EARLIER THAN THE RISE
of Christianity, but our great collections of Midrashim are rooted in
the period of early Christianity, the period of the New Testament.

The Midrash is a creative exegesis and understanding of the text
of the Bible and its stories, an attempt to discover all the various
senses implicit in the biblical verse. The word "midrash" already
appears in the Bible, but in a different sense. It appears clearly for
the first time in the Dead Sea Scrolls, where the Midrash is also
called *Pesher* (commentary). There are Midrashic works composed
by Essenes, and they even include a passage explicitly called
"Midrash."

Jewish Midrash is one of the expressions of Jewish creative
activity during the periods of the Second Temple and the early
Rabbinic literature. It appears that all the books of the New
Testament and all those persons who were active during the period
of early Christianity also had an affinity to the world of the
Midrash. The New Testament contains whole Midrashim, and it
also has, especially in the sayings of Jesus, allusions to Midrashim,
whether these specific Midrashim have reached us or not. There
are also typically Christian Midrashim, which set out to demonstrate the truths of Christianity from verses of the Bible. Jesus'

death and the belief in his resurrection and in his divine origin are explained through Midrashim which were created by Christians of their own accord or which originated in Jewish Midrashim.

Jesus himself had a profound Jewish education, and it is obvious that he was familiar with numerous Midrashim. The Gospels contain no explicit Midrashim, but only allusions to them. Jesus did not wish to burden his audience, some of whom were not educated, and therefore only hinted at Midrashim. Although he did not develop new Midrashic techniques, he had his own Midrashic method, using only the most subtle references to Midrashim which already existed at his time.

Even at the beginning of the Sermon on the Mount, we already have a hint to Midrashim: "Blessed are the poor in spirit, for theirs is the Kingdom of Heaven: Blessed are the meek, for they shall inherit the earth." It is obvious that the second of these verses is taken from Psalms 37:11: "But the meek shall inherit the earth," with the addition of the words "blessed are," whereas the first is a Midrash on "the meek shall inherit the earth." Jesus takes the word "meek" (Hebrew *anavim*) to mean the poor (Hebrew *ani'yim*) in spirit, on the authority of verses in Isaiah (57:15; 61:1) which speak of the meek and the humble in spirit; and he explains in a Midrashic manner the expression "they will inherit the earth" in the sense of "theirs is the Kingdom of Heaven."

In Matthew 5:21 ff., Jesus explains in a Midrashic manner the commandment "Thou shalt not kill" to imply that one should not be angry. In this Midrashic manner he extends the meaning of "Thou shalt not kill" by applying the Midrashic principle of *a fortiori*.

In the first Gospels we also find Midrashim on Biblical verses, which are sometimes not part of Jesus' sayings. If the New Testament explains that Jesus' sufferings correspond to those of the Servant of the Lord in Isaiah 53, this is a Midrash, adapting the Biblical passage to Jesus. The New Testament contains Christian Midrashim whose aim is to show that the stories of the Bible were fulfilled in the life of Jesus. Thus these Midrashim are used as evidence for the truth of the stories about Jesus, and especially to explain the disaster of his death. The story of Jesus' death sets out to overcome the disappointment of his followers after his execution, which was to all outward appearances the failure of his movement. In this case, the early Christians attempted to find Biblical verses which hinted that this catastrophe was not unforeseen.

One of the problems arising in relation to the study of the Midrashim, and especially those found in the Pauline Epistles and the other Epistles of the New Testament, is the scarcity of Midrashic texts of that period, except for the Dead Sea Scrolls. It is true that there are isolated Midrashim dating from that period, but the final redaction of Midrashic collections is very much later. Hence the special importance of the New Testament, which shows that even in that period there were already in existence sophisticated forms of Midrashim.

In our Jewish collections of Midrashim, a certain Midrash is sometimes taken out of its context; part of it is to be found in one place and part of it in another, in the same collection or in another collection. Since these collections were put together during the period of the Tannaim or even later, during the period of the Amoraim (the later Talmudic Sages, from about 200 to about 500 C.E.) or even after their time, one can never know what was the precise original extent of a single Midrash. From the New Testament we learn that there were already far more complex Midrashim than we would have imagined if we had not had the New Testament. In these Midrashim, various Biblical verses which had some similarities between them were combined. Once a conclusion was drawn from one of them, it was possible to pass on to another verse for an additional proof of what had been said in the first, and thus some long Midrashim were created in the New Testament. This shows that this method was already employed by the Sages and the Biblical exegesis of that period.

The literature of the Sages began to be collected in the generation following the destruction of the Temple. Thus we can find parallels to New Testament Midrashim only in very late collections. The sophisticated Midrashim in the Dead Sea Scrolls and in the

New Testament Epistles, though, are a proof of the existence of sophisticated and complex Midrashim as early as the period of the Second Temple.

There is, of course, the possibility that a late Midrash similar to one found in the New Testament or in the writings of Philo of Alexandria was independently deduced later for the second time, without drawing from the earlier source. It is thus advisable to check every instance in its own right. If a Midrash which has been observed in a late Rabbinic text has the same structure and the same approach as the Midrash found in the New Testament, we may assume that that Midrash did, in fact, originate in the days of the Second Temple. We are not always as lucky in drawing parallels as in the case of Paul's words in Romans 12:15: "Rejoice with them that do rejoice, and weep with them that weep." In *Tosephta Berakhot* 1:21 we read: "Hillel the Elder said: "Do not appear... to be laughing, and do not appear to be weeping, for it is written, 'A time to weep and a time to laugh.'" Hence this Midrash on Ecclesiastes 3:3 was already quoted by Hillel, who was earlier than Paul.

The Epistle to the Hebrews attempts to demonstrate that Jesus is the Messiah, that he is greater than Abraham (7:7), than the angels (1:4) and than Moses (7:7). A parallel, later Midrash is found in *Tanhuma* (Buber's edition, *Toldot* 134–135; Vulgar edition, *Toldot* 14). The Midrash is on Isaiah 52:13: "Behold my servant shall deal prudently, he shall be exalted and extolled, and be very high." The Messiah will be more "exalted" than Abraham, more "extolled" than Moses and more "high" than the angels. This Midrash is found in a late collection; but it is clear that the Epistle to the Hebrews proves that it had existed already at the time of the Second Temple or soon after its destruction. The antiquity of this Midrash is also demonstrated by a Tannaic Midrash, namely *Sifre*, on Numbers 12:3-7. There, Rabbi Jose says that Moses is greater than the Patriarchs and the angels. Hence originated the Midrash which attempted to prove that the Messiah is greater even than Moses, than the Patriarchs, including Abraham, and the Archangels. This is a Midrash we find in both Tanhuma and the

Epistle to the Hebrews in the New Testament. It is interesting that a medieval Jew who converted to Christianity, Friar Paul Christiani, noticed the affinity between the *Tanhuma* Midrash and the Epistle to the Hebrews and tried to prove on this basis, and on the basis of other problematic arguments, that the Talmudic Sages had known the Christian truth, but had concealed it from the Jews. In his disputation with the Jewish Rabbi Nachmanides, this convert to Christianity said: "Indeed, your own Sages have said of the Messiah that he has more honor than the angels, the which cannot be but of Jesus." He then quoted what was written in the Midrashic legend: "Exalted and extolled and very high: exalted more than Abraham, extolled more than Moses and higher than the Archangels." Nachmanides, of course, had his answer ready to hand. (*The Writings of Rabbi Moses ben Nahman*, Chavel's edition, Vol. I. p.311.)

We conclude that Jewish Midrashim were employed in the New Testament to portray the image of Jesus as the Messiah. Some of them were not specifically related to Jesus and his destiny, and some came to explain his execution and to support the belief in his resurrection. Once the Christians had learned the technique of the Jewish Midrash, they also invented their own Christian Midrashim; first, using the Hebrew text of the Bible, and later using even the Greek translation of the Law and the Prophets.

The obvious conclusion is that the writers of the books of the New Testament employed for their own needs Jewish Midrashim dealing with the Messiah as a sublime figure, and this is evidence for the fact that such Midrashim had existed in a very early period.

Another problem is the relationship between Jews who wrote Greek and the Palestinian Midrash. The writings of Philo of Alexandria, who lived during the period of the New Testament, have been studied, and the question has been raised as to what extent Philo was dependent on ideas and methods of exegesis current in Greek thought, and to what extent he was dependent on Palestinian materials.

Midrashim which appear in the New Testament and in rabbinic sources sometimes also appear in works written in Greek. Scholars who were not familiar with Palestinian Midrash believed these works, especially the works of Paul, were influenced by the allegorical, Midrash-like exegesis current in the Greek world. But from the Dead Sea Scrolls and from the Jewish Midrashim it becomes clear that even Midrashim written in Greek, which tell us sublime stories and see their own times as reflected in the Bible, are close to the Jewish Midrashim both in content and in their reconstructed original form, or are even taken straight out of the treasury of Hebrew Midrashim.

As for rabbinic parables in the New Testament, they are to be found solely in the mouth of Jesus. This specific literary form, created by the Sages of Israel and typical of the literature of the Sages, was already known to Jesus, and he continued to develop it. From a comparison of the parables of the Sages with the parables of Jesus it appears that this literary form was already highly developed at the time of Jesus. The first parable we have in a fully developed form is a parable of Rabban Yohanan ben Zakkai, a few decades later. It appears that Jesus sometimes introduced some modifications in parables he had heard from others, and other times simply handed on parables such as those we find in the writings of the Sages. Thus in some cases we can date some of the parables of the Sages a few hundred years earlier than their present form.

From the New Testament we learn of great intellectual and literary achievements which had already been attained during the generations before Jesus. The New Testament reflects these achievements and is genuine evidence of this flowering of literature and culture.

XI.

Paul and the Dead Sea Scrolls

PAUL, ONE OF THE MOST IMPORTANT OF THE FOUNDERS OF Christianity, is probably the most famous early Christian besides Jesus. Many regard him as the second founder of Christianity. Paul did not know Jesus. He was a citizen of Tarsus, in Asia Minor, and according to one piece of information which has reached us (Jerome, *About the Famous Men*, Chapter 5), his family originated in Gush Halav in Galilee. He was an observant Jew, and defined himself as a Pharisee. Paul came to Jerusalem, as did other Jews who came there from the Greek-speaking diaspora; he wanted to persecute the Christians, and received a letter of recommendation from the High Priest to act against the Jewish Christians in Damascus. On the way to Damascus, Paul had a vision of Jesus. He changed his attitude and way of life and became a Christian.

Paul lived in a state of tension with the Christian community of Jerusalem, all the members of which were observant Jews. He developed his own particular doctrine, or gospel, which took no account of Jesus' own preaching, but considered the core of Christianity to consist of the act of salvation by Jesus the Messiah who redeemed the whole of mankind and opened the gate, as it were, to the Gentiles. Paul's attitude to the Torah and the commandments was in no way positive, and this attitude was an indirect cause of the Christians' rejection of the Torah and commandments.

Paul was thus regarded as the second founder of Christianity. His knowledge of Judaism was meager compared with Jesus', but Paul was familiar with Hellenistic Judaism, and he had also absorbed information from Christian circles about other trends of Judaism.

Like every new religion Christianity developed stage by stage. In its first years, this development was extremely fast. Even before Paul launched his activity as a Christian, Christianity had already spread not only among Palestinian Jews, but also among Jews in the diaspora. From comparisons between the Dead Sea Scrolls and Paul's Epistles, we can learn much about the way in which Christianity developed, as well as about the influence of Essene doctrines on Christianity in its incipient stages.

It appears that both the Gospel according to John and the Epistle to the Hebrews, as well as some other Epistles of the New Testament, represent a second stratum of Christianity, as against the first one, that of Jesus and his disciples. The first stratum of Christianity had special affinities with Rabbinic Judaism, whereas the second stratum, from which Paul sprang, was influenced by the Essenes and their world-view. The Essenes, through channels which are unknown to us, influenced Hellenistic Jewry in Asia Minor and other countries. These Hellenistic circles were an important factor in the later disengagement of Christianity from Judaism.

As against the Essene influence on Jesus, which was not of a religious nature but was restricted to his admiration for poverty, there was an Essene influence on Hellenistic Judaism, and through it on Christianity, precisely in issues concerned with the nature of religious faith. Among the findings of Qumran, there is but one piece of evidence for the links between Hellenistic Jewry and the Essenes. In one of the Qumran caves, only the remains of Greek writings were discovered. This is evidence of a library for disciples of the Essenes who came from Greek-speaking countries. One should also remember that the Jewish Pseudepigrapha, including those which show affinities with the Essenes, were translated into

The flight of Paul from Damascus, *from a ninth century manuscript.*

Greek.

The people of Qumran had a dissenting theology, and it is precisely this element of dissent which was later a moving force in Christianity. The Essenes separated themselves from the evil world: they were the Sons of Light. In the second stratum of Christianity, the Christians were called Sons of Light. The Dead Sea covenanters thought that against them stood the rest of Israel and the other nations as Sons of Darkness. According to them, there is a long drawn-out conflict which will culminate, in the end of days, in a war – the War of the Sons of Light and the Sons of Darkness. The Scrolls also endow great prominence to the Devil, who is called, among other names, Belial, and whose counterpart on the side of the Sons of Light is the Archangel Michael. By means of such ideas, whose origin is perhaps Persian, the people of the Scrolls justified their separation from the world around them, their dissenting attitude towards the rest of Israel, and their consciousness of being God's only chosen people.

In order to explain the nature of the divine grace which had elected the Sons of Light and which was active even before the creation of the universe, the people of the Scrolls devised a concept of a double predestination: what God has decreed at any time is inalterable; God determined who is going to be the righteous and who will be the wicked. A man has been elected before he joins the community. He is God's elect, and he has to confirm this election through his actions.

Man is in mortal sin from the day of his birth until his final day, and God raises His elect above that mortal sin. The elect constitute, as it were, a spiritual temple, as against the unclean Temple of Jerusalem, and they atone for the sins of the world.

Because of their dissent, the Essenes regarded themselves as the people of the new covenant. They believed that it was this new covenant which their forefathers had broken, as is in Jeremiah 31:31. That is, the new covenant was identified by the people of this sect with the covenant one struck when one joined the sect. The expression "new covenant" (or "new testament") never appears in sayings of Jesus. Christianity is thus the new testament, standing up against the first covenant, the Torah of Moses, but with far greater tension than we find in all the doctrines of the Essenes.

Such doctrines penetrated some Hellenistic Jewish circles, whose existence can be deduced from an examination of the affinities between the Pauline and similar writings and the Dead Sea Scrolls. The new community inherited the belief in its own election by divine decree, and of the election of each individual Christian by divine grace. The individual was elected by divine decree before the creation of the world, and anyone who was not elected was condemned to everlasting abhorrence. In Christianity, divine grace does not come about through the covenant of the sect, but through the sacrifice of Jesus, which becomes the sacrifice of the new covenant (testament). From the Essene belief that a man could not improve his ways since he was in a state of the sin of flesh and only God's grace could make him into an elect, Paul drew the conclusion that God's election was the only act of grace, and that there was no point in fulfilling the commandments of the Torah, since they did not lead to divine grace.

In the Essene world, which was strict in its adherence to the commandments, there was a contrast between the sinning flesh and the saving spirit. Paul and his associates, on the other hand, regarded the commandments as part of the realm of the flesh. The commandments were actions of the flesh. They were of no use; they merely increased the pride of the man who pretended to be righteous by fulfilling them. Paul claimed that it was only divine grace which elected a man; the commandments were practically abolished, and were even considered to contain an element of evil.

Although the Essenes regarded the Temple with some tension, they hoped for its restoration once it fell into their hands and was purified in the future war of the Sons of Light and the Sons of Darkness. They conceived the image of the community as a spiritual temple, consisting of the members of the sect – a conception similar to that of the Christian Church. In this manner, the Essenes overcame the difficulty caused by their belief in the uncleanness of the Temple, as against their special pride in being a separatist sect.

and an institute of the holy spirit. This element, too, entered the Pauline books of the New Testament and the second stratum of Christianity, and was thus accepted as an image of the Christian community.

To sum up, the Scrolls are a primary source for the views of the second stratum of Christianity and of Paul. These views passed through further modifications in Christianity. Through the confrontation between the Scrolls and the second stratum of Christianity, the influence of the Essenes on some circles in Hellenistic Judaism is also revealed.

XII.

Hellenistic Jewry

THE JEWS OF THE HEBREW–SPEAKING DIASPORA WERE A FACTOR which exercised some influence on the transformation of Christianity into a religion of the Gentiles. These Jews spoke Greek, and their literary creation was in Greek. In those days a sense of the emptiness of polytheistic beliefs and of the moral corruption of mankind was widespread throughout the world, and there was a growing sympathy for the Jews and for their attitude to religion. Many people joined Judaism as full proselytes, and others, who were called "God–fearing," did not take upon themselves the full yoke of the Commandments, but undertook to keep some of the obligations of Judaism. Such men were the first to join Christianity as a result of the preaching of Paul and his sect.

Most of our sources concerning Hellenistic Jewry come from Alexandria. Some scholars believe that Christianity reached Egypt only at the end of its first stage, toward the end of the second century C.E. We do not possess much information about Hellenistic Jewry in other parts of the diaspora. Alexandrian Jewry is largely reflected by the Jewish-Greek philosopher Philo of Alexandria, and because of the great interest shown in his writings, people have concerned themselves far less with Hellenistic Jewry in other countries.

In a way, Philo of Alexandria is not a representative figure in Hellenistic Jewry – not even in Egypt itself, and even less so outside Egypt. Philo of Alexandria was the son of a rich family. His brother supplied the Roman Imperial family with funds. Philo's acquaintance with Judaism was meager, and yet he stepped forth as a Jewish philosopher. Philo exercised a great influence on Christianity in the age of the Church Fathers, but one can hardly detect his line of thought in the New Testament – an identification of Judaism with philosophy and a conception of the Jew as the true citizen of the world. Philo's writings abound in symbolical and allegorical interpretations of the Scriptures, although he was familiar mainly with the Pentateuch and knew only a smattering of the other books of the Bible. Thus, Philo's approach to Scripture is of no help for the understanding of Hellenistic Judaism, whose way was different from his and from that of his friends. For the understanding of Hellenistic Judaism, the books of the New Testament offer us indirect help.

The Hellenistic Jews did not belong to the higher strata of society. The language in which the New Testament as well as the Greek Bible and certain Greek-Jewish works were written was a popular, vulgar language, familiar to us from papyrus letters discovered in Egypt and written by ordinary people. No Gentile literature was written in that popular language, except for parts of Hellenistic Jewish literature and the books of the New Testament.

Only authors like Philo did not write their books in that popular language. This shows us that most of the Hellenized Jews were not, in general, particularly well educated. They showed no interest in the classics of Greek literature, and what they knew of Greek philosophy they learned from popular works and from the discourses of philosophical preachers.

Not only the Jews, but the other nations which had gone through a process of outward Hellenization, were not especially learned. Paul, a Jewish artisan, attempted to some extent to familiarize himself with Greek culture for the sake of his mission; but his Gentile neighbor, most probably a shoemaker, knew nothing of the message of Greek culture.

During the early period of Christianity, Jews resided not only in Egypt but in all parts of the diaspora: Asia Minor, Syria, Italy, Spain and other areas. The Jews of the West were also Greek-speaking, just as, later on, Gentile Christian communities spoke Greek.

Certain circles of Greek-speaking Jews were greatly influenced by the Essenes. The Jews of the diaspora felt that they were in constant danger of anti-Semitism, and were faithful to Palestine. They were not equal to the Gentiles in their legal rights, and their hope for redemption was nurtured mainly by conflicts with anti-Semites. There were times when the Gentiles respected the Jews, but at other times they accorded them their most profound hatred.

The Hellenization of many nations was never completed, for we know that once classical culture became extinct, many of these nations returned to their pristine language. In Syria, a Syrian literature in Aramaic was created, and in Egypt, ancient Egyptian gave rise to the Coptic language. The Jews had their own culture, based on Scripture, and mainly on the Pentateuch. Many of them knew Hebrew, especially those who spoke Aramaic besides Greek. But there were also Jews who knew only Greek, and they studied the Torah and read it in Greek translation in their synagogues. The Greek Septuagint translation of the Bible was also studied by Gentiles who had a close relationship with Jews.

The Hellenized Jews visited the Temple. They also founded in Palestine their own synagogues, as we are told in the New Testament. It is true that their knowledge of Judaism could not be compared with that of the Palestinian Jews, and their children did not receive as good a Jewish education as did the children of Palestinian Jews, but they did remain loyal to Judaism, and one can take it that most of them kept the commandments – at least to the extent to which they were familiar with them. Perhaps it was this fulfilling of the commandments on a soil which was not part of their motherland which aroused in them a sense of insecurity and suspicion. They were, for example, suspicious of Paul. It was these Hellenized Jews who persecuted Paul and who brought about his arrest by the Romans when he visited Jerusalem. The tension

Philo, from a ninth century manuscript.

Philo and Josephus, **from a ninth century manuscript.**

◄ *Philo, from a ninth century manuscript.*

between Paul and the Hellenistic Jews was great, since they were terrified of a new faith which could have shaken their Jewish faith to its foundations.

Hellenistic Jewry accepted with joy the achievements of Palestinian Jewry. It is well known that Palestinian Sages, like Rabbi Akiva and his pupil Rabbi Meir, visited the countries where they were settled, and so did other Aramaic- or Greek-speaking Jews.

In Philo's writings, we can sometimes discover Jewish homilies which the Alexandrian preachers had learned from Palestinians. Philo adapted such Midrashim according to the particular method developed in Greek philosophy for the exegesis and reinterpretation of Homer. Sometimes one can detect Palestinian elements in Philo's writings as well. In those works of the New Testament which were written originally in Greek by Hellenistic Jews, the immense impact of Palestinian materials is evident. It is clear that even people who knew no Hebrew were influenced by the sermons of the Sages. The phenomenon of Midrashim as part of the exegesis in the books of the New Testament and of epistles written by Jews as part of Hellenistic Jewish or Christian literature is well known. Such Midrashim were frequently interpreted by scholars who had no idea of the nature of a Midrash and were familiar only with Philo. They believed that what they found was the influence of Greek philosophy and Greek diatribes, and that the Biblical verses were interpreted, as it were, by the symbolic methods of Greek-Jewish philosophy.

This claim, that a Greek influence was at work here, is incorrect. On the contrary, most of the Midrashim and the Midrashic parallels have been preserved in the New Testament precisely in the writings of Christians of Jewish origin.

It is true that Philo gave great prominence to an entity which he named "logos," the word of God by means of which He created the world. But the word through which the world was created also appears in Jewish Midrashim from Eretz Israel. This entity, which was later identified with Jesus, was developed by Philo through philosophical exegesis, but it is also one of the achievements of Jewish thought in Palestine. When the Hellenized Jews lived at some distance from Palestinian Jewry and had no Jewish schools, they developed mystical tendencies and an inclination towards supernatural entities like the Word – and this tendency is reflected especially in those Christian works of the New Testament which originated in a Hellenistic Jewish milieu.

To sum up, Hellenistic Jewry served as an instrument for the transmission of the new faith to the Gentiles. At the same time, Paul was suspect, not only in the eyes of the Hellenized Jews themselves, but also, and for other reasons, by the Palestinian Christians. The New Testament presents us with the possibility of the existence of Hellenized Jews who opposed Judaism, and among whom the elements of strife and heterodoxy were rife even before they went over to Christianity. These Jews spread Christianity, and at the same time they transmitted to the Gentiles some of the values of Hellenistic Judaism. One should not see in all those who spread the Christian faith Jewish heretics.

XIII.

Jesus' Jewish Disciples and Their Followers

JESUS WAS A FAITHFUL JEW. HIS PERSONAL DISCIPLES AND THEIR followers who resided in Palestine were Jews who had studied the Torah and were strict in their observance of the commandments.

As against the Gentiles who accepted Christianity, these disciples regarded Jesus as a great prophet and as the Messiah. These were Jews who despaired, for a brief moment, of their faith in Jesus the crucified, and who regained their faith through their belief in his resurrection. They were usually simple people, often poor, and they passed on the sayings of Jesus. They were not all that interested in the divine Christ, but rather in the historical Jesus, the prophet who had dwelt amongst them.

In its struggle against Gentile Christianity, Jewish Christianity emphasized the Judaism of Jesus. In all the Jewish-Christian writings which have reached us, Paul appears as a villain. All the various groups and trends of Jewish Christianity were united in speaking against Paul. Some of them adopted Peter, Jesus' disciple and the leader of the first Christian community in Jerusalem, as their patron. Some preferred James (Jacob), Jesus' brother. James was executed by the Sadducees, and it was the Sages who had opposed his execution and supported him. Thus James became the founding father of Jewish Christianity or Hebrew Christianity, as against the Messianic Christianity among the Gentiles, which developed, according to the Hebrew Christians, mainly because of Paul's desire to increase his own power.

The Jewish Christians are known to us not only from the New Testament but also from some Christian Apocrypha. Professor Shlomo Pines has discovered an early source in an Arabic adaptation made in the tenth century which proves that the last groups of such Jewish Christians were still in existence in the tenth century C.E.

One can detect traces of their principal beliefs and even discover whole works of theirs in an adapted form in Christian literature of the period of the New Testament onward. The Jewish Christians interpreted the issues of Christianity in their own way and according to their own traditions and information. It is clear that some of their materials, adapted to suit the interests of the Church, have penetrated into the ecclesiastical literature of Gentile Christianity. These Jewish Christians were persecuted by the Church and regarded as infidels and heretics who had gone the wrong way and had attempted to Judaize Christianity. It was said of them that their world-view was deficient, and that they did not comprehend the divinity of Jesus.

At the same time, Jewish Christianity was not all homogeneous. Not only did the disciples and followers of the Christians who lived in Jerusalem and in the Galilee continue in their way, but there were also other Jewish groups, with different views, who joined Christianity. One of those groups was the Ebionites. Their literature has been partially preserved in ecclesiastical adaptations. This was a small sect with peculiar and eccentric views. Its members were vegetarians, and their vegetarianism originated in their opposition to sacrifices, and perhaps to the slaughter of animals altogether. They were opposed to the service in the Temple in Jerusalem, and believed that the Jews were commanded to offer sacrifices as a punishment for the Golden Calf. They believed that true Judaism had no sacrifices, and that the Scriptures were forged,

Jesus crucified, with Longinus piercing his left side. On his right are Mary and John. On the extreme left, Judas hangs on a tree, with thirty pieces of silver at his feet.

The tomb of Jesus in the Holy Sepulcher, as it appears in a work by B. Von Briedenbach, 1483.

The tomb of Jesus in the Holy Sepulcher, as it appears in a work by B. Von Briedenbach, 1483. (chapter Thirteen)

with the sections dealing with sacrifices interpolated at a later period. The Ebionites accepted the Jewish view which we find in the Scrolls concerning the existence of three prominent figures: the Messiah Priest, the Messiah the Son of David, and the Prophet of the End of Days, and they attempted to find out whether Biblical prophecy was true prophecy.

The Ebionites lived in expectation of the Messiah, and they believed that on his coming their views concerning the forged sections of Scripture would be confirmed, the sacrifices in the Temple would be abolished, and spiritual worship would take their place. According to their belief, the entity of the Messiah had traversed the generations, from Adam through the great men of Israel until it had found its resting place in Jesus, in whom it had materialized.

Out of the Ebionites there sprang a peculiar prophetic sect. Around 100 C.E., there existed in Mesopotamia a group of Ebionites who expected the second coming of Jesus the Messiah. They upheld Messianic beliefs concerning the End of Days, and thought that they had received an additional revelation – a holy book delivered to a man called Heil Kasai (Aramaic for "hidden strength"), in the Greek form "Elchasai."

Around the year 200 C.E., the Manichean religion was a serious candidate for the position of a world religion. This religion had spread from North Africa to India. Its founder was Mani, who lived in Persia under the Sassanid King Sapor I. His father, Patak, was for many years a member, together with his son, of the Erchasaite sect, whose ideas exercised an influence on the Manichean religion.

Manicheanism spread in many areas, and Augustine the Church Father was for a while one of its followers. He had no idea that that strange religion of vegetarians who wanted to bring about the redemption of the world had originated in Jewish Christianity, of all things.

The first Jewish Christians, the disciples of Jesus, reached a state of conflict with Paul, who held a position of strength compared with the Christians of Jerusalem. Paul hardly spoke to the

Jerusalem community, and he, so to say, set up Christ the Savior against the historical Jesus.

The Jews were suspicious of Paul, not only because of his position concerning the commandments, but also because he adopted the Gentiles into his community with such ease. The Jewish Christians and other Jewish groups joined them in their suspicions. Among others, the sect which preceded the Ebionites, known as the Nazirites, also joined them. Certain other groups which lived in a state of tension toward their Jewish brethren turned to Christianity once the Jews had refused to accept their views. During the Roman Wars, the Jewish Christian groups emigrated to Fella across the Jordan, and later on they returned to Jerusalem. After the Second Jewish Revolt, they were not permitted to reside within Jerusalem, because they were Jews. Then the heads of the community who were circumcised emigrated to Lebanon.

Kaukaba was a center for Jewish Christians of all the various streams – for those who were closer to the Church, as well as for those who were closer to Judaism. From the second century onward, Christianity forbade the Jewish Christians to keep the commandments and persecuted them as heretics. Because of this persecution, a growing opposition to the Gentile Church spread among the Jewish Christians. The Jewish Christians were reminded of their Judaism and began to feel an increasing sense of identification with the people of Israel. They claimed that Paul, Peter, and even James had been driven by an instinct for power, and therefore had adapted themselves to the ways of the Gentiles. They criticized the three in the same manner as later Jewish literature, maintaining that because of Christianity's turning towards the Gentiles due to impure motives, it had lost the chance of being accepted by the Jews. Unlike the Gentile Christians, who faced east in their prayers, the Jewish Christians continued to face the ruined Temple in the Holy City of Jerusalem. They maintained that the proper language of teaching, in which the early Gospels had been written, was Hebrew, and that, when the Gospels had been translated into other languages it was as though they had been forged. Since they rejected the Pauline Epistles, they created their own Gospels according to traditions of their sects and ancient traditions which had reached them. These Gospels, some remains of which have reached us, were an act of the Judaization of the extant Gospels.

We have surveyed the ideological, social and organizational flowering of the Jewish Christians and their influence on Christian religious literature. The Jewish Christians were rejected by the Jews and persecuted by the Christians, who regarded them as heretics and villains. Despite all this, Christian literature reflects their creative vitality and their loyalty to Judaism. Because of ecclesiastical censorship, only some relics of their own writings have reached us. But the faithfulness of the Jewish Christians to Judaism, despite all their difficulties, is worthy of admiration.

Bibliography

1. The collected papers of David Flusser will soon be published by Magnes Press, Jerusalem.
2. About the beginning of Christianity, see the two books of Y. Krausner, *Jesus* and *From Jesus to Paul.*
3. About rabbinic thought, see especially the following books:
   - S. Schechter, *Aspects of Rabbinic Theology*, N.Y.: Schocken Books, 1967.
   - Büchler, *Types of Jewish Piety*, N.Y.: KTAV, 1967.
   - A. Büchler, *Studies in Sin and Atonement*, N.Y.: KTAV, 1967.
   - E.E. Urbach, *The Sages*, Jerusalem: Magnes Press, 1979.
4. About the Dead Sea sect and origins of Christianity, see especially:
   - D. Flusser, "The Dead Sea Sect and Pre-Pauline Christianity," *Scripta Hierosolymitana* IV, "Aspects of the Dead Sea Scrolls" (1958), pp. 215–266.
   - D. Flusser, "Blessed are the Poor in Spirit," *Israel Exploration Journal* 10 (1960), pp. 1–13.
   - S. Safrai and D. Flusser, "The Slave of Two Masters," *Immanuel* 6 (1967), pp. 30–33.
   - D. Flusser, "The Last Supper and the Essenes," *ibid.* 2 (1973), pp. 23–27.
   - D. Flusser, "The Hubris of the Antichrist in a Fragment from Qumran," *ibid.* 10 (1983), pp. 31–37.